DECADES OF THE 20th CENTURY

IN COLOR

THE 1990s

FROM THE PERSIAN GULF WAR TO Y2K REVISED EDITION

STEPHEN FEINSTEIN

Library of Congress Cataloging-in-Publication Data

Feinstein, Stephen.
  The 1990s from the Persian Gulf War to Y2K / Stephen Feinstein.—Rev. ed.
    p. cm. — (Decades of the 20th century in color)
  Includes index.
  ISBN-10: 0-7660-2639-6
    1. United States—Civilization—1945– —Juvenile literature.
  2. Nineteen nineties—Juvenile literature. I. Title. II. Series:
  Decades of the 20th century in color.
  E169.12.F444 2006
  973.92—dc22
                                        2005019877
ISBN-13: 978-0-7660-2639-1

Printed in the United States of America

10 9 8 7 6 5 4 3

To Our Readers: We have done our best to make sure all Internet addresses in this book were active and appropriate when we went to press. However, the author and the publisher have no control over and assume no liability for the material available on those Internet sites or on other Web sites they may link to. Any comments or suggestions can be sent by e-mail to comments@enslow.com or to the address on the back cover.

Illustration Credits: AP/ Wide World Photos, pp. 4, 12, 19 (top), 21, 23, 29, 31, 34, 35, 37-39, 45, 47, 48, 50, 53, 57, 58; Deidre Davidson/Saga/Archive Photos, p. 25; Enslow Publishers, Inc., pp. 9, 19 (bottom), 20; Fotos International/ Archive Photos, p. 28; Getty Images, p. 6; JupiterImages Corporation, pp. 10, 11, 18, 55; Reuters/Emil Vas/Archive Photos, p. 44; Reuters/Fabrizio Bensch/Archive Photos, p. 24; Reuters/Gary Hershon/Archive Photos, p. 26; Reuters/HO/ Archive Photos, pp. 14, 27, 41; Reuters/Jim Hollander/Archive Photos, p. 49; Reuters/Joe Giza/Archive Photos, p. 32; Reuters/Lee Celano/Archive Photos, p. 15; Reuters/Mike Theiler/Archive Photos, p. 40; Reuters/Peter Andrews/Archive Photos, p. 43; Reuters/Rick Wilking/Archive Photos, p. 13; Reuters/Sam Mircovich/Archive Photos, p. 17.

All collages composed by Enslow Publishers, Inc. Images used are courtesy of the previously credited rights holders.

Cover Illustration: Archive Photos (individual photographers credited above).

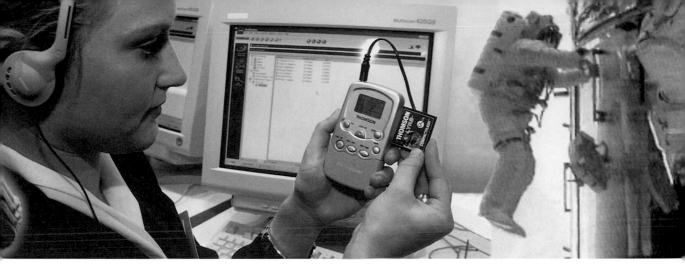

Contents

Despite the optimism at the end of the 1980s, after the Berlin Wall (above) came down and communism fell, the 1990s were a time of turmoil for much of the world.

Dawn of a Decade

The 1990s began on an optimistic note. The Berlin Wall had just been torn down late in 1989, bringing a symbolic end to the forty-five-year-long Cold War between the United States and the Soviet Union. After the fall of the wall, the Communist governments of Eastern Europe fell, too, one by one. In 1991, the Soviet Union itself collapsed. Russians then began the difficult process of changing their nation into a democratic society. Now that the Cold War was over, Americans could look forward to peace. But the world would not be a peaceful place in the 1990s. The United States would go to war in the Middle East, and take on the task of policing the world as the only superpower.

In spite of these problems, the 1990s proved to be a period of prosperity for many Americans. The United States had its greatest boom economy in post–World War II history. Perhaps the biggest changes in the economy and society came about through the development of the Internet.

Depending on the size of the document to be downloaded from the Internet, the information would appear on the user's computer screen in anywhere from a few seconds to minutes or longer. This gave birth to the expression "World Wide Wait."

Information Overload

During the 1990s, the Internet brought a whole new world right to people's fingertips. It was the world of cyberspace, often called the Information Superhighway. In an instant, anyone with access to a computer, modem, and telephone line could connect to huge databases anywhere in the world. With a few simple mouse-clicks, powerful search engines would retrieve information from the World Wide Web. Scientists and engineers worked constantly to find ways to make information pass faster over the Internet.

Online, a person could read magazines, news articles, encyclopedia entries, even entire books. Such information was available any time, day or night. Before long, some people felt they were drowning in information.

Of course, having so much information available did not necessarily mean it was all accurate or good. Easy access to the Internet meant that almost anyone—even those with faulty information or dangerous motives—could post sites for the public to view.

Only a Mouse-Click Away

The Internet brought a new way to communicate with people. E-mail was easy. Often it was more convenient and cheaper than using the telephone. A person could send an e-mail message at any time of day or night without fear of disturbing the recipient, who could respond when it was convenient.

Another Internet function that became extremely popular was the chat room. People could have ongoing discussions with all kinds of people. Since the true identity of participants was usually unknown, many people invented their own online personalities, identifying themselves by a code word. Although this secrecy helped protect Internet users' privacy, it also led to new dangers. Now criminals could approach their victims and win their trust—all under a fake name.

Many hailed the Internet for its great success in easing communication. Advocates claimed the Internet was bringing Americans closer together. Yet, more and more Americans were suddenly spending countless hours alone, staring at their computer screens. It was often said that the Internet simultaneously brought people together and kept them apart.

Shopping Online

By the end of 1999, more than 40 million American households were on the Internet. Large numbers of people had begun shopping online. Amazon.com was the largest online retailer to emerge during the 1990s. Jeff Bezos, the founder of Amazon.com, started by selling books online. As Amazon's name became more widely known, Bezos began offering music CDs and videos. Later, Amazon began selling toys. Teaming up with other companies, Amazon was soon selling everything

from lawn mowers to pet supplies to prescription drugs. By decade's end, however, Amazon.com had yet to earn a dime in profit. Only time would tell if such an Internet business model—which carried enormous costs for startup and advertising—would work.

The Internet made possible new ways of buying and selling. A company called Ebay began to host online auctions. Another company, Priceline.com, allowed people to bargain for the best prices on items such as airline tickets, hotel room reservations, and groceries. Soon, traditional companies began to move onto the Internet. A growing number of Americans even began doing their banking and paying their bills online.

As more Americans logged on to the Internet, some people worried that records of a person's net surfing and shopping habits could be viewed by organizations such as

New types of computer equipment such as laptops (right) made it possible for people to take their work with them wherever they went. Growing numbers of Americans who had regular jobs either worked part of the time or all the time outside the office.

online advertising agencies and marketing companies. Online privacy became a controversial issue by the end of the decade, especially because of the fear that thieves could get access to credit card numbers and use the information to destroy someone's financial standing.

The Dot-Com Craze

Thousands of people took the Internet craze a step further and started their own businesses on the Web. A new career was created. Known as Webmasters, these people knew how to design, create, and maintain Web sites. Inspired by new Internet businesses such as Amazon.com, people frantically tried to borrow money for their businesses. Many raised huge sums. Quite a few Internet companies eventually sold stock to eager investors. Before long, the media was full of stories about the new dot-com millionaires. Many of them were young men and women in their twenties. By the end of the decade, however, very few of these new companies were making profits. They were spending lavishly on marketing, and cash reserves were beginning to dwindle. It seemed that the boom of Internet business could not last forever, and that a reversal of fortune would soon occur.

The Cell Phone

Toward the end of the 1990s, the use of cellular telephones rose dramatically. An increasingly common sight on city streets was a person walking along, chatting into a cell phone held up to his or her ear. It often seemed as though people were talking to themselves, oblivious to the fact that other people could not help but overhear their conversations.

Unfortunately, more Americans were also carrying on phone conversations while driving. Because this habit was

Sleek little cellular phones were snapped up by millions of Americans—who could not seem to put them down once they bought them! It would not be unusual to see a couple seated at a restaurant, with one or both of them talking into a cell phone rather than speaking to each other.

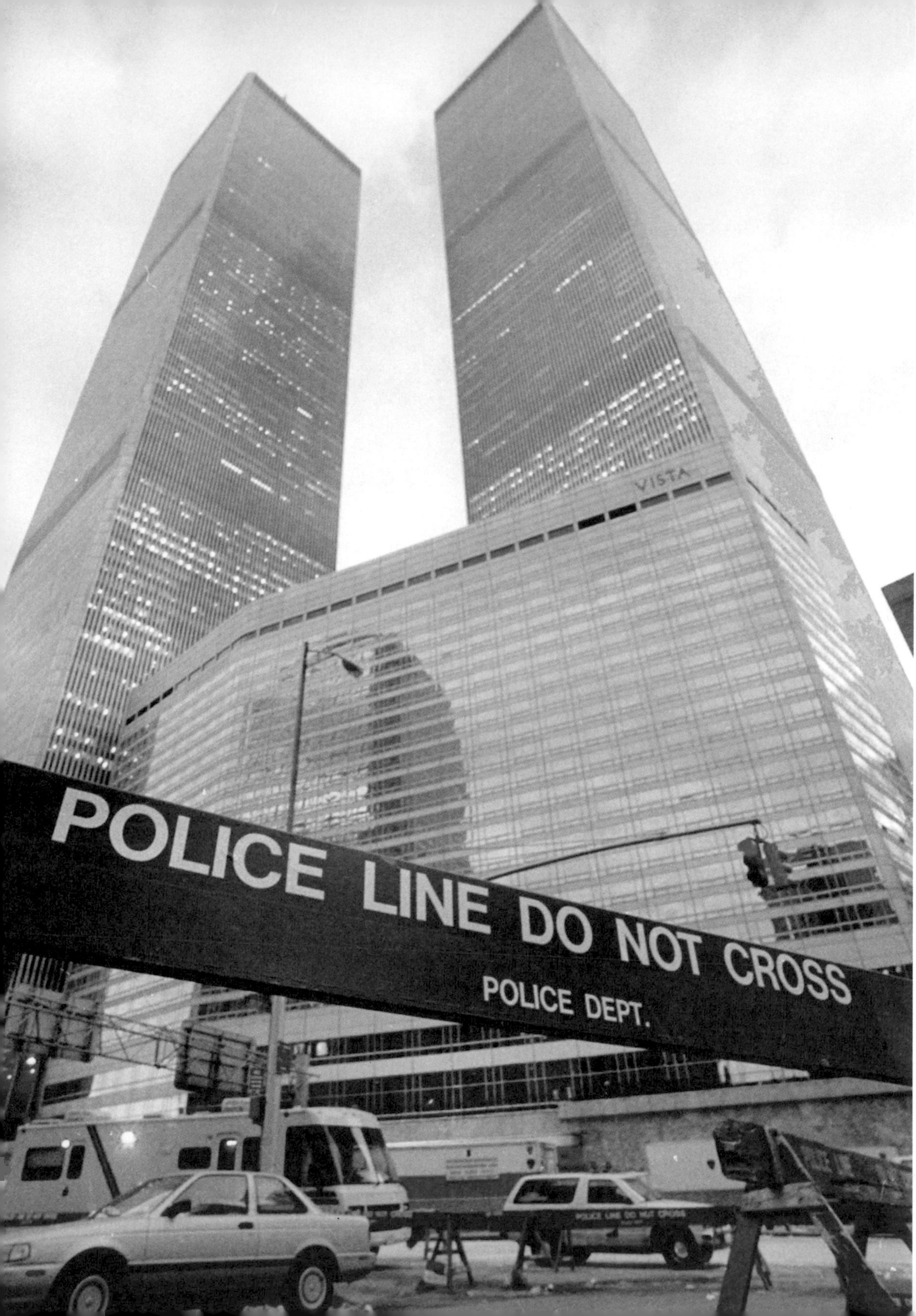
VISTA
POLICE LINE DO NOT CROSS
POLICE DEPT.

dangerous and caused frequent accidents, some towns passed laws against using cell phones while driving.

Terrorist Bombers

The nation was shaken to the core during the 1990s by the actions of terrorists who caused horrific suffering. In February 1993, Muslim terrorists set off a car bomb at the World Trade Center in New York City, killing six people and injuring more than a thousand. (Eight years later, on September 11, 2001, terrorists would succeed in completely destroying the World Trade Center.)

Another unbelievable episode occurred on April 19, 1995. Timothy McVeigh, a decorated army veteran with ties to right-wing militia organizations, used a powerful truck bomb to blow up the Alfred P. Murrah Federal Building in Oklahoma City, Oklahoma. The bombing killed 168 men, women, and children, and injured hundreds more.

Then, there was the case of Theodore Kaczynski, who came to be known as the Unabomber. Kaczynski believed that technology was going to destroy the world. To prevent this from happening, he mailed homemade letter bombs to people he considered a threat, including college professors and scientists. Kaczynski managed to kill three people and injure twenty-nine others before he was captured.

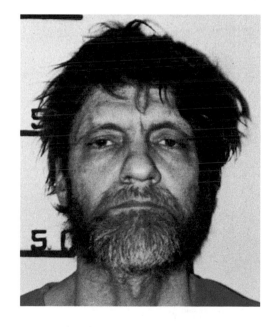

In 1995, a terrorist attack in Japan gave Americans something new to worry about. In that incident, twelve people

The actions of those intent on creating havoc made Americans aware of their vulnerability as citizens of a free society. Terrorists, like those who bombed the World Trade Center for the first time in 1993 (opposite) or the Unabomber (below), had just as much freedom of movement as any other person.

were killed and more than five thousand injured when members of a cult called the Aum Shinrikyo released deadly nerve gas into the air vents of a Tokyo, Japan, subway station. If such a terrible attack could happen in Tokyo, Americans feared it could also happen in the subways of New York, Boston, or Los Angeles.

Teen Assassins

The Columbine shootings killed thirteen people (eight of the victims are seen below).

The behavior of terrorists was hard to understand. Even harder to understand were several shootings that occurred in American public schools. Within a two-year period, there were five mass school shootings in the United States.

The worst incident occurred at Columbine High School in Littleton, Colorado, on April 20, 1999. Two students, Dylan

Cassie Bernall   Corey Depooter   Lauren Townsend   Daniel Mauser

John Tomlin   Matthew Kechter   Rachel Scott   William "Dave" Sanders

Klebold and Eric Harris, burst into the school and went on a rampage. They killed twelve students and a teacher before killing themselves. The two young killers had belonged to a group whose members wore long black trench coats and called themselves the Trench Coat Mafia. Apparently, the two young men had spent much of their spare time playing violent computer games. Many observers believed Klebold and Harris were so alienated or so emotionally immature that they could not distinguish between the real world and the virtual reality of computer games. Or perhaps the two just wanted to make a name for themselves. At any rate, after the shootings at Columbine, the safety and well-being of the nation's school-children suddenly seemed to be at great risk. It was clear that a lot more attention needed to be paid to any teenager who seemed to be having emotional problems. Some places also took steps—such as installing metal detectors and carrying out locker searches— to keep dangerous weapons out of schools.

Eventually, cases like Rodney King's (below) caused politicians to demand an end to the practice of "racial profiling," in which people would be stopped and questioned by police solely because of their skin color.

"Can't We All Just Get Along?"

These were the words of Rodney King, an African American who was beaten by police in 1991. King was responding to the horrifying outbreak of racial violence in Los Angeles in 1992 during what was possibly the worst race riot in United States history. By the time it was over, fifty-five people had been killed, more than four thousand injured, and more than twelve thousand arrested. More than five thousand buildings had been destroyed or badly damaged. The riot was ignited by the not-guilty verdict in the trial of four white police officers who had been videotaped as they beat King during a traffic violation arrest.

Cases of police brutality against minorities added to the atmosphere of mistrust between the whites who made up the majority of law enforcement officers and African-American and Hispanic-American citizens. Even by the end of the decade, unequal treatment by the justice system remained a sad reality of daily life for many minorities.

In California, a weak economy contributed to a growing racist backlash against the large number of illegal aliens, about 7 percent of the population, mainly from Mexico. Recent immigration laws had failed to stem the tide of illegals crossing the border. In 1994, California voters passed Proposition 187 (59 percent voted "yes"). The new law denied health care, welfare, and public education to illegal immigrants and their families.

The Trial of the Century

The most glaring example of America's racial divide was the opposing responses of blacks and whites to the O. J. Simpson trial. African-American football hero and movie actor O. J. Simpson was accused of murdering his former wife, Nicole Brown, and her friend Ron Goldman, both of whom were white. The two had been found gruesomely stabbed to death in June 1994. Though he claimed his innocence, Simpson was arrested and brought to trial. The whole nation became almost obsessed with the trial. There was unprecedented daily television coverage, and many Americans remained glued to their televisions, as if they were watching a soap opera.

Much circumstantial evidence seemed to point to Simpson's guilt, especially DNA evidence. But Simpson's attorneys portrayed their client as a victim of a racist white justice system.

The jury found Simpson not guilty. In a startling contrast, 85 percent of African Americans agreed with the verdict, while only 32 percent of whites did. The case showed not only the racial tensions in America, but economic problems as well. Simpson was a wealthy man who could afford world-class attorneys. Many believed he was able to buy his way out of trouble. However, a later civil trial found him responsible for the deaths of his ex-wife and Ron Goldman, and forced him to pay huge sums in damages.

Casual Workdays

During the 1990s, many fashions were recycled from previous decades. The grunge look that began in the late 1980s was still popular with teens, while some rappers and hip-hoppers

Key to the defense in the murder trial of O. J. Simpson in 1994 was a white police officer, Mark Fuhrman, who had collected the blood evidence from the crime scene. Fuhrman's credibility was damaged when he was caught lying about having used racial slurs in the past.

continued to wear oversized clothes, with pants hanging low around their hips. Pierced eyebrows, noses, and other body parts were popular, as were ragged jeans with holes in them. Tattoos on various parts of the body were more popular than ever. Even retro items such as miniskirts and bell-bottoms could often be seen.

In the business world, more people were dressing casually. The trend had started with "casual Fridays," the one day of the week on which many companies allowed employees to come to work without their usual formal business suit.

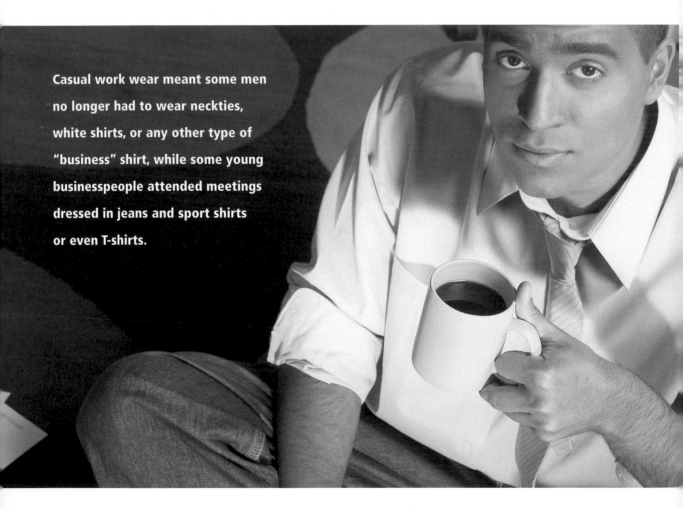

Casual work wear meant some men no longer had to wear neckties, white shirts, or any other type of "business" shirt, while some young businesspeople attended meetings dressed in jeans and sport shirts or even T-shirts.

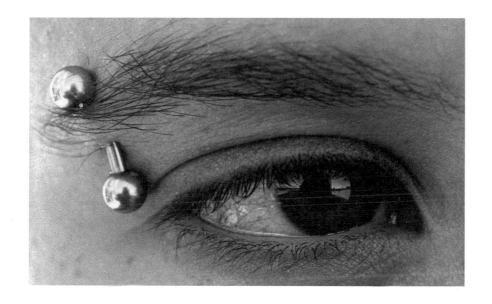

Perhaps the new casual attitude had something to do with the dot-com companies, where it was hard to find an employee over the age of thirty. But increasingly, in dot-com companies as well as in some older companies, casual Fridays were being extended to every day of the week. Increasingly, the same outfits were appropriate for both work and play.

Must-Have Toys

Throughout the 1990s, several fads erupted that would rival the hysteria caused by novelties of earlier decades,

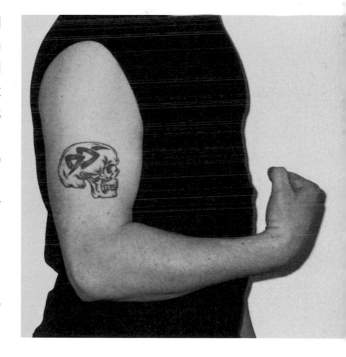

such as the pet rock of the 1970s or the Cabbage Patch Kids of the 1980s. Most of these fads were children's toys, and they made both parents and children embark on mad searches to find the newest and rarest items.

Beanie Babies were one of the toy crazes of the decade. People of all ages frantically purchased and traded the stuffed toys, trying to add to their collections.

Among the most popular toys of the 1990s were Beanie Babies—small animals filled with bean-bag stuffing. Beanies came in all shapes, sizes, and colors, and they were marketed as collector's items. Many American households owned dozens—if not hundreds—of the Beanies. Finding new—or better yet, rare or retired—pieces was all the rage. Fast-food chains got in on the action, too, giving away miniature Beanies with children's meals. These promotions often caused long lines and rapid sell outs. Some companies even began to produce Beanie-related merchandise, such as storage bags or special shelves to hold the valuable Beanie collections.

Other toy fads included the Furby: a furry, though not quite identifiable, creature specially equipped with electronics that enabled it to speak, move, and perform other pet-like functions. Children all over America became almost obsessed with "feeding" or otherwise caring for their Furbies. Some teachers found the toys so distracting that they were forced to confiscate them—at least until the end of the school day.

Death of a Princess

One of the most tragic events of the 1990s happened on August 31, 1997. England's Princess Diana, who had only a year earlier been divorced from Charles, the Prince of Wales, was killed in a car crash in Paris, France. Known as the People's Princess, Diana had long been a symbol of glamour and style, but she was also well-known for her work with many different charities. Despite her break with the British royal family, Diana was seen as a caring, affectionate mother and a great humanitarian who had lent a touch of charm to British royalty. Coverage of Diana's funeral and moving tributes to her life had people glued to their televisions the world over.

The death of Princess Diana was one of the most tragic events of the 1990s.

Searching for an Alternative

Like fashion, musical styles from previous decades refused to go away in the 1990s. Every possible variety of music attracted its own following. The sophisticated lyrical harmonies of groups such as Boyz II Men and 'N Sync were popular with music lovers who sought beauty and sweetness in their music, as well as with young girls who considered the male vocalists heartthrobs. Equally popular were hip-hop and gangsta rap, which appealed to fans who liked the anguished cries of the city street being set to rhythm. Superstars from earlier decades, such as Sting and the Rolling Stones, also remained popular, both with older people and with young people to whom they were a fresh new sound.

Many young people were searching for a musical style to call their own. In the early years of the decade, some found it in the music of Kurt Cobain and his band, Nirvana. Cobain's music cried out for a rejection of all that was bland and slick in American culture, including the prevailing styles of pop music. Young people responded to Nirvana's rebellious spirit. The music, characterized by loud guitar distortion, became known as alternative music. However, loud, harsh-sounding rock music was hardly a new sound. Punk rockers and heavy metal groups had been creating such musical "noise" for many years. The spirit of rebellion had also been an element of rock music for decades. At any rate, Nirvana became an overnight sensation.

One of the most artistically and commercially successful bands of the 90s was Nirvana, led by Kurt Cobain. Unfortunately, Cobain could not seem to handle his success. He committed suicide in 1994.

Music Meets the Web

The term *alternative* was applied to so many different artists and groups that it eventually became meaningless. In one sense, however, it pointed to new developments. The growth of the Internet made possible a whole new way of producing and distributing music, as well as listening to it. Small independent, or "indie," labels had managed to produce albums over the years, in the shadow of the major music companies, with varying degrees of success. Now, with the Internet, it became possible for anyone to become an independent producer. A musician could put his or her own music on the Web, and anyone with access to the Internet could easily download the music. Thus was born a true "alternative" to the major labels. By the end of the

New technologies such as MP3 allowed the transfer of music files with CD-quality sound over the Internet. A company called MP3.com made use of MP3 technology to provide online access to hundreds of thousands of music tracks supplied by mostly small, not-yet-well-known music acts in search of publicity. MP3.com also allowed users to load their own private music collections into a personal "locker" they could access from any computer over the Internet.

decade, the big recording companies were grappling with the issue of music piracy, as previously copyrighted music became available to download for free.

One company, called Napster, let its users "swap" their music at no cost over the Internet. Any recorded song was available for free to Napster's 20 million users. The major labels, alarmed at the prospect of losing enormous sums of money, took legal action against Napster and other companies.

Edgar Bronfman, Jr., head of Universal, the world's biggest music company, said that soon "a few clicks of your mouse will make it possible for you to summon every book ever written in any language, every movie ever made, every television show ever produced, and every piece of music ever recorded." Clearly, the major music labels—as well as book publishers and other corporations—would have to find a way to function alongside the expanding Internet.

"Living La Vida Loca"

Following in the foot-steps of Cuban-American singing sensation Gloria Estefan and Panamanian-born singer Rubén Blades, other Latino musicians traveled the "crossover" route in the 1990s, recording music that appealed to both Hispanic and non-Hispanic Americans. Their flashy videos featured the fancy footwork of sensual dancers. Singer Ricky Martin thrilled millions of fans with his passionate endorsement of a wild and crazy lifestyle. Singers Marc Anthony and Christina Aguilera also attracted a wide following.

Probably one of the most amazing musical developments involved a group of elderly Cuban musicians who had performed at the Buena Vista Social Club in Havana about fifty years earlier. American guitarist Ry Cooder, an avid fan of Cuban music, visited the island to record and jam with Cuban musicians. He located some of the Buena Vista musicians who were living in poverty and obscurity, not having performed for many years. Seventy-two-year-old lead singer Ibrahim Ferrer, for example, now shined shoes for a living. Cooder brought the musicians together, organized recording sessions, and produced an album and a movie about the musicians and their music. The project was successful beyond anyone's wildest

One of the biggest stars to emerge out of the late 90s was Jennifer Lopez. Popularly known as J-Lo, she found great success as both an actress and a singer.

The focus on Hispanic crossover artists, including Ricky Martin, led many non-Hispanic music fans to discover the exciting world of salsa music for the first time.

dreams. It resulted in worldwide fame for the musicians of the Buena Vista Social Club and concerts in places such as New York's Carnegie Hall.

Seeing Is Believing—Or Is It?

Like everything else in the 1990s, moviemaking made extensive use of cutting-edge computer technology and new digitalization techniques. In 1993, director Steven Spielberg produced *Jurassic Park*. It became an instant hit with moviegoers who were thrilled by the dinosaurs thundering across the screen. The prehistoric creatures were so startlingly "real" that it was hard to believe actual dinosaurs had not been captured on film.

Taking technology a step further, *Toy Story* (1996) was the first feature-length animated film created entirely by computer. It revolutionized the art of animation. Similar films soon followed, including *Antz* and *A Bug's Life*.

In music videos and some films, a technique called morphing made it possible to manipulate images of people in new ways. One person could even be transformed into another.

Computer technology was also used in the movie *Titanic* to convince audiences that the huge ocean liner they saw disappear beneath the waves on screen was the real ship *Titanic*. This disaster film became one of the biggest movie hits of all time.

Though he excelled at creating technologically advanced hits, Steven Spielberg also produced some great dramatic

Moviegoers were amazed by the effects of films such as *Antz*.

films during the 1990s. *Schindler's List* (1993) was a drama portraying the heroic deeds of Oskar Schindler, a German industrialist who rescued Jews employed at his factory from death during the Holocaust. In 1998, Spielberg produced the World War II drama *Saving Private Ryan*. It included an amazingly realistic depiction of the sheer terror experienced by American soldiers as they stormed ashore on the beaches of Normandy, France, during the D-Day invasion of Europe.

Shows About Nothing

One of the strangest developments in entertainment during the 1990s was the popularity of so-called "shows about nothing." Steering away from sitcoms with off-the-wall plots, some new television programs began to try to depict characters with problems and interests like those of real people. Among the most popular new shows was *Friends*, which centered on the everyday activities of a group of six friends in their twenties. Also popular was *Seinfeld*, which focused on the ordinary—although very comical—happenings in the lives of a group of New Yorkers. The shows avoided sweeping plot lines or unrealistic situations, trying instead to make everyday situations, such as conversations with friends, working, or dating, funny.

In 1999, TV viewers had a new way to watch their favorite shows

Many teenage girls went to see *Titanic* again and again, drawn by young heartthrob Leonardo DiCaprio as much as by the incredible special effects in the film about the doomed ship.

about nothing—or something. That year, The TiVo company introduced a home version of the digital video recorder (DVR). Using this device, a viewer can pause a program and resume it later without missing any part of it. One popular feature allows the viewer to watch a show commercial-free.

TV viewers who enjoyed watching movies at home by either renting or buying videocassettes also had a new way to enjoy movies. In 1997, DVDs (digital versatile or video disks) became widely available. DVDs had superior sound and image quality as compared to videocassettes.

Shows like *Friends* (above) and *Seinfeld* were extremely popular during the 1990s. Also popular were reality-based programs that tried to show people as they really live and work. Among these were *ER* and *NYPD Blue*.

Tigermania

In previous decades, golf appealed mainly to rich people. Typical golfers were businessmen trying to maintain good relationships with colleagues and clients. Deals were often made over a friendly round of golf. During the 1990s, some 3.2 million new golfers—mostly younger men and women in their twenties and thirties—took up the sport.

One person who was responsible for the sudden increased popularity of golf was the amazing young professional golf champion Eldrick "Tiger" Woods. In 1991, Woods became the youngest winner of the United States Junior Amateur championship. He captured that title again in 1992 and 1993. He turned professional in 1996, winning two Professional Golf Association (PGA) titles that year and being named the PGA Tour's outstanding rookie. As Woods's popularity grew, more new golfers rushed to try their own hand at the sport. Fans admired Woods's incredibly powerful long shots as well as his expert putting.

Born in 1975, Tiger Woods wasted no time getting into golf. It soon became clear that he was born to play the sport. At the age of two, he appeared on a television program swinging a golf club. At the age of three, he shot an incredible score of 48 over nine holes. It was onward and upward from there.

In 1997, Woods became the first African-American golfer to win the Masters Tournament. He shot a record 270 over 72 holes and finished 12 strokes ahead of the rest of the players. In 1999, he won eight PGA tournaments in one year, becoming the first golfer in more than two decades to do so. During the 1999–2000 season, Woods earned more than $6 million in prize money for his winning streak of six consecutive victories. The champion golfer was now a rich man although, partly thanks to his fame, golf was no longer just a rich man's sport.

Record Breakers Bring Back the Fans

In August 1994, major-league baseball players went on a strike that lasted until the following spring. Not only were baseball fans deprived of the last part of the 1994 baseball season, but the strike also caused the cancellation of the World Series. Fans were outraged. When the 1995 baseball season started late, many angry fans stayed away from the games. Baseball stands stood nearly empty throughout the 1995 season.

Slowly, though, fans went back. Americans loved baseball too much to hold a grudge forever. And a few emerging champions were causing excitement. In 1996, the Baltimore Orioles' "Iron Man," shortstop Cal Ripken, Jr., broke Lou Gehrig's record of playing in 2,130 straight games. From 1982 through 1996, Ripken played in 2,216 consecutive games. Fans grew even more excited during the 1998 season when not one but two ballplayers broke Roger Maris's 1961 record of 61 home runs in one season. Mark McGwire of the St. Louis Cardinals hit 70 homers, and Sammy Sosa of the Chicago Cubs hit 66. Unfortunately, allegations of steroid use in later years would cast doubt on the legitimacy of these home run records.

Baseball made a huge comeback during the 1990s, thanks largely to the talent of players like Cal Ripken, Jr. (above).

Scary Moment at the Olympics

An incident at the 1996 Summer Olympics reminded Americans, who were still shaken by the 1995 Oklahoma City bombing, of the danger of terrorism. Atlanta, Georgia, had been selected to host the Summer Games. No expense was spared to put on the most extravagant Games in the history of the Olympics.

Huge crowds flocked to Atlanta. Unfortunately, among them was someone who was up to no good. A pipe bomb exploded in Olympic Park, killing two people. Earlier, a security guard named Richard Jewel had found and reported a mysteriously abandoned backpack. He was arrested and wrongly accused of the bombing. After a long investigation, he was released. The true bomber has never been found, although federal authorities continue to pursue possible suspects. Unfortunately, the violent incident overshadowed the Olympic Games themselves, in which the United States won a total of 101 medals, 44 of them gold.

Extreme Athletes

During the 1990s, a growing number of American athletes were drawn to challenging kinds of activities called extreme sports. Not content to ski down slopes that were considered difficult by most skiers, for example, extreme skiers skied down vertical cliffs, sometimes dropping considerable distances in free fall before landing on the snowy slopes below. Such skiing seemed to be thrilling—for those who survived!

Another extreme sport was long-distance rowing. Tori Murden, a thirty-six-year-old Kentucky lawyer, is a member of the Sector No Limits Team. This group of athletes is dedicated

Pictured are competitors from the 1996 X Games, Chris Senn (in the Skateboarding Street Finals) and Robert Vasiluth (in the Bungy Jumping Compulsary Competition).

to testing the limits of human endurance. Not content to row across a lake or river, Murden set her sights on the Atlantic Ocean. Murden proved to be perhaps the most persistent rower of all time. She had tried and failed to row across the Atlantic twice in 1998. Her boat capsized fifteen times during Hurricane Danielle and she had to be rescued. Finally, in 1999, she became the first American—and the first woman—to row three thousand miles across the Atlantic Ocean. She survived being tossed into the sea when twenty-foot waves during Hurricane Lenny caused her twenty-three-foot-long boat, *American Pearl*, to stand on end. Throughout the voyage, Murden avoided loneliness by using a satellite phone to speak to friends and to send email messages to schoolchildren.

Tori Murden's successful voyage from the Canary Islands off the coast of Africa to Guadeloupe in the Caribbean Sea took eighty-one days.

Operation Desert Storm

In August 1990, Iraq's dictator Saddam Hussein invaded and occupied the country of Kuwait, asserting historical Iraqi claims to that land. Hussein's plan was to gain control of more of the Middle East's oil resources, which would help Iraq's economy. Once it controlled Kuwait, Iraq was a threat to Saudi Arabia, the region's major oil producer and an ally of the United States. George Bush, America's Republican president, had a background as an oil industry executive. He understood very well the importance of oil to America's economy. Bush declared, "This aggression will not stand."

Besides threatening oil supplies, Hussein was known to be developing weapons of mass destruction—nuclear, chemical, and perhaps biological weapons. Comparing Saddam Hussein to Adolf Hitler, President Bush assembled a coalition of thirty nations, including many Middle Eastern nations, and began Operation Desert Shield, a massive military buildup in the region. The United Nations immediately sent at least two hundred fifty thousand troops under the command of American General Norman Schwarzkopf. Within several months, that number had grown to more than half a million troops, mostly from the United States.

Operation Desert Storm began on January 16, 1991, when the United States and its allies began a campaign of air strikes against Iraq. Television viewers worldwide watched the bombardment of Baghdad, Iraq. Mindful of Americans' bitter memories of the nation's humiliating defeat in the Vietnam War and of all those who had died in vain during the 1960s and early 1970s, General Colin Powell and America's other military leaders in the Persian Gulf War, as Desert Storm came to be called, were determined to keep American casualties to a minimum.

After more than a month of bombings in which many innocent Iraqi civilians died, General Schwarzkopf began a ground invasion of Iraq on February 23. Within just one hundred hours,

Soldiers undergo chemical training in eastern Saudi Arabia during Operation Desert Shield in November 1990.

Ironically, the United States had provided Saddam Hussein (above, in a video still) with supplies of advanced weaponry during the Iran-Iraq War, fearing that an Iranian victory would threaten the West's access to Saudi oil.

the Persian Gulf War was over. More than one hundred fifty thousand Iraqi soldiers and civilians were killed, along with 141 American soldiers. Kuwait had been liberated from Iraqi control. The threat to Middle East oil had been eliminated, although Iraqi forces set fire to Kuwait's oil fields as they fled the country. Saddam Hussein was allowed to remain in power, although he continued to cause problems for the rest of the decade.

"It's the Economy, Stupid!"

Just after the Persian Gulf War ended, Americans gave George Bush an approval rating of 91 percent, the highest ever for an American president. Yet, just one year later, America had slipped into an economic recession. Bush's popularity slipped dramatically. Bush had reluctantly agreed to raise taxes, breaking his 1988 campaign pledge: "Read my lips, no new taxes." Bush fought a losing battle in the 1992 presidential election. The Democrats, with their rallying cry, "It's the economy, stupid!" blamed Republican economic policies for ruining the nation's economy. Democratic candidate Bill Clinton, the governor of Arkansas, and his running mate, Al Gore, said they were "new" Democrats, not the old "tax and spend" liberals. A third presidential candidate, Texas billionaire H. Ross Perot of the Reform party, provided lively and folksy analyses of what was wrong with the two major parties, but he won little support when the votes were counted. In the end, Clinton was elected president.

The Clinton administration proposed sweeping changes right from the start. First Lady Hillary Rodham Clinton took on the task of reforming America's health care system. Health care reform, however, did not go far, and at the end of the decade, 37 million Americans were still left without health insurance.

Minorities in Government

During his campaign, Bill Clinton had promised to hire women and minorities for important government positions. He fulfilled that goal. African American Ron Brown became commerce secretary, and Hispanic American Henry Cisneros became housing and urban development secretary. Janet Reno became America's first woman attorney general, Donna Shalala became secretary of health and human services, African American Jocelyn Elders became surgeon general, Ruth Bader Ginsberg was appointed to the United States Supreme Court, and women headed the Council of Economic Advisers and the Environmental Protection Agency. In 1996, Clinton appointed Madeleine Albright as the nation's first woman secretary of state.

Colin Powell's political career was founded on his military successes in the first Gulf War in 1991.

The Siege at Waco

Attorney General Janet Reno faced criticism for her handling of a cult situation just over two months after entering office.

On April 19, 1993, more than eighty people—members of a cult called the Branch Davidians—died after setting fire to their housing compound in Waco, Texas. Back on February 28, government agents tried to serve cult leader David Koresh with a warrant. Koresh and his followers had responded with gunshots, killing six federal agents and wounding sixteen. Six Davidians had been killed. A standoff occurred, with the cult members refusing to surrender to federal agents. When the FBI moved to force the cult out of the compound after two months, Koresh decided to die and to take his followers with him. Many Americans blamed the FBI—and Attorney General Janet Reno—for the tragic deaths of the cult members.

The Clintons came under attack soon after they arrived in Washington. Many conservatives opposed them.

The Contract With America

In 1994, Republicans in Congress announced a ten-point "Contract with America" to promote the policies they stood

for. In part because of numerous controversies in which the president was involved, in the 1994 elections Republicans took control of both houses of Congress for the first time since 1954. Newly elected Speaker of the House Newt Gingrich led the Republicans in bitter battles against Democratic policies. Republicans were particularly angry about Clinton's $280 billion tax hike, the largest tax increase in America's history.

Although the economy had grown much stronger during Clinton's first term in office, Republicans partially shut down the government twice in a battle over the federal budget. Many Americans, however, still liked Bill Clinton. Inflation was down, family income was up, and unemployment had fallen to 5.6 percent. So in 1996, Americans reelected Clinton to a second term in office.

Presidential Scandals

American prosperity continued during Bill Clinton's second administration, but his presidency was undermined by scandal. In 1997, lawyers heard rumors about an affair between Bill Clinton and Monica Lewinsky, a twenty-two-year-old intern at the White House. Clinton, testifying under oath in another case in which he had been accused of sexual harassment, denied having sexual relations with Lewinsky. Meanwhile, a friend of Lewinsky's named Linda Tripp secretly recorded Lewinsky's emotional account of the affair with Clinton. Tripp then gave the tape to investigator Kenneth Starr. Attorney General Janet Reno approved Starr's request to investigate Clinton's possible lying under oath.

Despite the scandal over Monica Lewinsky and impeachment, Bill Clinton still enjoyed a 65 percent approval rating in the polls. In fact, it seemed that the impeachment procedure actually hurt Republicans more than it did Clinton.

Newspaper and television reports were filled with accounts of the alleged affair. Clinton declared on national television that he had not had a sexual affair with Monica Lewinsky. It soon became apparent that Clinton had lied. Clinton later apologized to the nation on television.

Republicans in Congress, along with some Democrats, condemned Clinton's behavior and began hearings to see if there were grounds to impeach the president (formally accuse him of wrongdoing). Eventually, Bill Clinton was impeached on two articles—perjury and obstruction of justice. Although having a sexual affair is not a crime, lying about it in court is. He became the second United States president (Andrew Johnson was the first), and the first elected president, to be impeached. If convicted by the Senate, he would have been removed from office. The Senate vote was 55–45 against conviction on the first article, and 50–50 on the second. A two-thirds vote was needed to remove the president, so Clinton survived the ordeal.

The Soviet Union Self-Destructs

In one of the most surprising political developments of the 1990s, the Soviet Union fell apart. For decades, America's spy agencies had grossly overestimated the strength of the Soviet economy. On August 19, 1991, Mikhail Gorbachev, the leader who had tried to reform the Soviet system, was almost overthrown by a group of political leaders who wanted to return to a strict Communist form of government. Boris Yeltsin, who was president of Russia, stood up on a tank in Moscow and defied the organizers of the overthrow. Commanders of key army units refused to order their troops to fire on the demonstrators in Red Square. The coup failed, and Gorbachev was returned to power. On August 23, the government suspended all activities of the Communist party. And on December 25, the Soviet Union was dissolved. All former member states of the Soviet Empire became independent. Gorbachev resigned because the Soviet Union he had governed no longer existed.

Throughout the rest of the decade, Russia and the other former Soviet republics struggled to reform their economies and become more democratic. Russian leader Boris Yeltsin faced huge problems. Russia's transition from a planned economy to

a free market economy was marred by corruption. Currency was dangerously devalued, and life became difficult for most Russians, who wondered if they had not been better off under communism. In 1993, Yeltsin had to send troops and tanks to put down a revolt by former members of the legislature. To add to Russia's woes, in 1994, a disastrous war with separatists in Chechnya, who were struggling to secede from Russia, ended inconclusively. By decade's end, the war had resumed.

The Butcher of the Balkans

Back in 1914, the Austrian Archduke Franz Ferdinand had been assassinated in Sarajevo, the capital of the Balkan republic of Bosnia, setting off World War I. In the 1990s, the Balkans

Boris Yeltsin (above, center, wearing suit) became immensely popular for his role in ending the 1991 coup attempt. After the Soviet Union was dissolved, Boris Yeltsin continued as president of Russia, exerting great influence on world affairs.

Often referred to as the "Butcher of the Balkans," Yugoslav ruler Slobodan Milosevic started four wars during the 1990s in his determination to hold on to power at any cost.

once again became the setting for bloodshed, torture, and murder. Many of these troubles were caused by one man—the "Butcher of the Balkans," Slobodan Milosevic.

When the Communist regimes of Eastern Europe fell in 1990, and Russia itself abandoned communism in 1991, Yugoslavia's Communist leader Milosevic, who had risen to power in the late 1980s, saw the writing on the wall. When various states of Yugoslavia—Slovenia, Croatia, Bosnia (Bosnia-Herzegovina), and Macedonia—one by one declared their independence, Milosevic found himself in charge of a much smaller Yugoslavia, made up of only Serbia and Montenegro. He seized on nationalism as a force to replace communism. He planned to create a "greater" Serbia, by extending Serb control over parts of Croatia and Bosnia. Playing upon ancient ethnic and religious hatreds, he whipped up support among the Serbs for wars of aggression against their Balkan neighbors.

In 1991, the Yugoslav Army attacked Slovenia, but was quickly repelled. Milosevic then launched an attack against Croatia. Croatian strongman Franjo Tudjman put up a fierce resistance. Serbian citizens of Croatia were caught in the middle and suffered along with the Croatians.

More than elsewhere in Yugoslavia, Bosnia seemed to have achieved a true multiethnic society. Bosnian Muslims, Serbs, and Croatians had been living in peace and harmony for many years. But in 1992, Bosnian Serbs, under the leadership of Radovan Karadzic, with the strong support of Milosevic, began a campaign of "ethnic cleansing." Suddenly, old friends and neighbors turned against each other. Entire populations of villages were driven out of Bosnia, and in many cases, massacred. The capital city of Sarajevo was frequently bombed by Serb forces in the surrounding hills. Much of the city was destroyed, and many of its citizens killed.

By 1995, Milosevic realized that he would not succeed in reclaiming Bosnian and Croatian territory. United Nations peacekeeping forces had for the most part been unable to

Serbian children wait on line for lunch in the village of Tulari in September 1992.

protect Bosnian citizens, but United Nations sanctions were causing serious problems for Yugoslavia's economy. The Serbs also faced pressure from other nations. In 1994, American jet fighters shot down four Serbian jets over Bosnia. And in 1995, the Croatian Army expelled Serbs from traditional Serb enclaves in Croatia.

Milosevic traveled to Dayton, Ohio, where, on behalf of the Bosnian Serbs, he signed a peace agreement ending the war with the Bosnian Muslims and the Croatians. American peacekeeping troops were sent to Bosnia, where they would be stationed for years to come.

Kosovo

In 1998, a long-standing feud between the Serbs and ethnic Albanians in the southern Serbian province of Kosovo developed into an armed conflict between Serbian police forces and the Kosovo Liberation Army (KLA). The KLA sought independence from Serbia. In 1999, Slobodan Milosevic launched a full-scale military operation in Kosovo. Once again, his strategy consisted of ethnic cleansing. Entire villages were burned and their inhabitants forced out or killed.

The United States and its allies feared that the instability of Albania, Kosovo, and Macedonia could spread to surrounding countries such as Bulgaria, Greece, and Turkey. This might trigger a general war in the southern Balkans. To stop Serbian aggression, the United States and its allies began air strikes over Kosovo and Serbia in March 1999. Nine hundred targets, including the Yugoslavian capital city, Belgrade, were bombed. By June, there had been a total of thirty-two thousand bomber missions. Serbian forces had been driven out of Kosovo, and the war ended.

Africa and the End of Apartheid

Ethnic differences were at the root of many of the wars that erupted in Africa during the 1990s. By far the worst episode of ethnic violence occurred in 1994 in the nation of Rwanda. There, the Hutu people, who made up 80 percent of the population, greatly outnumbered the Tutsi, but had been dominated economically by them for many years. Hutu government officials organized and began a policy of genocide against the Tutsi. The Hutu-dominated army went on a two-month rampage, butchering more than eight hundred thousand Tutsi people.

In South Africa, however, the 1990s brought remarkable political progress. During the 1980s, the United States and many other countries had imposed trade restrictions in an attempt to end that nation's policy of apartheid, or separation of the races.

In 1990, South African President F. W. de Klerk took the first steps toward ending the country's isolation. In February, he

In many places, the African continent was plagued by war, disease, and famine throughout the 1990s. AIDS continued to spread throughout the region, affecting men and women equally.

freed Nelson Mandela, the heroic freedom fighter who had been in prison for twenty-seven years. He also legalized the African National Congress (ANC), which had been fighting against the apartheid policy of South Africa's white rulers for decades. More progress quickly followed as the government began to repeal the nation's apartheid laws. In 1992, white South Africans voted to end rule by the minority whites by 1994. In 1993, de Klerk and Mandela shared the Nobel Peace Prize. And in 1994, in South Africa's first fully free elections, Mandela became the nation's new president, and de Klerk became vice president. In 1996, South African lawmakers passed a new democratic constitution, guaranteeing equal rights for all citizens, although the nation continues to face economic and political problems caused by the transition.

The spirit of cooperation between black Africans under the leadership of Nelson Mandela (above, with his wife, Winnie) and white officials led by F. W. de Klerk was an inspiration to social and political activists around the world. After decades of terrible racial discrimination, South Africa was finally making strides toward ending the policy of apartheid.

New Hopes for Peace in the Middle East

For true peace to prevail in the war-weary Middle East, Israel and the Palestinians would have to come to terms agreeable to both sides. The territory controlled by Israel is of great religious importance to the parties involved—the Jews of Israel and the Muslim Palestinians and Arabs. Those who wanted peace in the region were encouraged by developments in 1993. President Bill Clinton hosted peace talks in Washington, D.C., between Israeli leader Yitzhak Rabin and Palestinian Liberation Organization (PLO) leader Yasir Arafat. The two signed peace accords, outlining areas of agreement and a timeline of issues that needed to be negotiated before the

At the end of the peace talks, the two Middle Eastern leaders—Yasir Arafat (left, center) and Yitzhak Rabin (far left)—shook hands, an encouraging symbolic gesture that was seen on television by millions around the world.

signing of a final peace agreement. Among the provisions of the accord was a plan for Israel to withdraw from the Gaza Strip and the West Bank, which the Palestinians would be able to govern themselves.

Sadly, in 1995, Rabin was assassinated by a Jewish religious fanatic. His tragic death showed how difficult it was to achieve peace in a region where many people on both sides have strong feelings against peace. By the end of the decade, the peace process had made some slow progress. Palestinians controlled most of the land in the West Bank and the Gaza Strip, which was designated to become the new Palestinian state. The most difficult issue left to be decided was the future status of Jerusalem—a city both sides claimed as their capital. The area remained politically tense through the end of the century, with riots and bloodshed continuing to occur.

Some people—known as survivalists—packed their bags and headed for shelter in the late 90s. There they joined others who had dug in years earlier in preparation for the disaster they believed would occur when 1999 became the year 2000. Some worried people simply stocked up on canned goods and other supplies.

Y2K: The Disaster That Didn't Happen

As the year 2000, also known as Y2K, approached, doomsayers of all sorts—from religious fanatics to people afraid of technology—began to predict the coming end of the world—or at least the collapse of civilization. They believed everything would stop working at midnight on New Year's Eve, 1999–2000.

By the end of the 1990s, the entire world was computerized. Many governments and other vital businesses could no longer function without computers. Unfortunately, computer programs written several decades earlier could not distinguish any year beyond 1999. The next date after December 31, 1999, that the computer could recognize would be January 1, 1900. Programmers had assumed that the defect would be corrected long before it became a problem.

According to the doomsday scenario, planes would fall from the sky (so few people scheduled flights on New Year's Eve), financial systems would collapse (so people were told to withdraw money from the bank and have cash on hand), and distribution systems would break down (so people were told to stock up on food and other supplies). Even scarier was the possibility that missiles armed with nuclear warheads might be automatically launched by computer error.

The world held its breath as New Year's Eve approached. In spite of widespread apprehension, spectacular New Year's extravaganzas with elaborate fireworks displays went off without a hitch in many of the world's major cities.

The Y2K disaster never happened. Financial institutions, major corporations, and government agencies had begun converting their computer systems several years earlier. They were well prepared for the coming of Y2K.

Billions and Billions of Planets

In the 1990s, astronomers learned that there are other solar systems—stars far out in space that have planets orbiting around them, just like our sun. Of course, nobody has actually seen these planets, because they are too far away. But unmistakable evidence for their existence has been discovered.

What the astronomers saw was a slight wobble in the movement of a star. A star known as Upsilon Andromedae, located forty-four light years from Earth in the Milky Way galaxy, is believed to have three huge Jupiter-like planets spinning around it. The planets' gravity tugs on the star, causing it to wobble.

Since the Milky Way galaxy contains more than 200 billion stars, scientists estimate that there could be many billions

of planets. To determine if there are other civilizations in the universe, a scientific effort known as the Search for Extra-terrestrial Intelligence (SETI), has been scanning the heavens. Some teams have used radio telescopes to look and listen for radio signals among the billions of radio frequencies flooding the universe. Other teams have used optical telescopes to look for signals in pulses of light from the stars.

Killer Asteroids and Comets

In 1980, physicist Luis Alvarez and his son Walter theorized that an asteroid or comet crashed into Earth about 65 million years ago. They had discovered a layer of iridium in the ground, a rare element that later was found to extend

An astronaut enjoys a spacewalk on the Hubble Space Telescope (above), more than 370 miles above the surface of Earth, in December 1999. With such technology as the Hubble, which was launched in 1990, astronomers may some day discover Earth-like planets. Perhaps some have intelligent life, but we may never know for sure.

around the world. The Alvarezes proposed that the iridium had been delivered to Earth by an asteroid. The asteroid's impact produced huge clouds of dust that hid the sun for several years, causing a mass extinction of many forms of life including the dinosaurs. In 1991, scientists pinpointed the site of the impact as the Chicxulub crater in the Yucatan in Mexico. Evidence at the site indicates that the asteroid must have been six to nine miles (10 to 15 km) in diameter, and it must have hit Earth at a speed of 93,000 miles per hour (150,000 km/h).

Scientists believe that other previous mass extinctions in Earth's history may also have been caused by asteroid or comet impacts. They also believe Earth will again be struck by a killer asteroid sometime in the future. And in July 1994, as if to demonstrate the potential danger to Earth lurking in the depths of space, astronomers witnessed the spectacular impact of the Shoemaker-Levy 9 comet into the planet Jupiter. This was the first time human beings witnessed a comet crashing into a planet. The awesome event on Jupiter served as a wake-up call to astronomers, who called for renewed efforts to find all the objects in space that could someday threaten Earth.

Global Warming Is Here

Although the issue is still widely debated, most scientists now believe that the world is, indeed, growing warmer. The 1990s were the warmest decade on record, and 1998 was the warmest year ever recorded. Huge sections of the Antarctic ice shelf broke off and began drifting in the surrounding ocean. At the North Pole, areas usually covered by ice all year long are now free of ice during the summer.

If steps are not taken to stop the warming trend, many scientists believe that, sometime in the twenty-first century, the sea level may rise. Coastal cities around the globe, where most of the world's population lives, will be hit hard by flooding and other related disasters.

The Human Genome Project

In December 1999, researchers involved in the publicly funded effort Human Genome Project announced that they had traced the chemical sequence of chromosome 22, one of the twenty-three sets of molecules that provide the genetic map for human life. Francis Collins, the scientist who headed the

Through the 1990s, the threat of global warming began to cause scientists great concern. Some wondered if the earth would someday become an unlivable desert.

project, said, "This is the first time that we've had a complete chapter in the human instruction book." Collins's researchers discovered the order of about 545 of the estimated 700 genes on chromosome 22, or about 1.1 percent of the genes in the human body. If these numbers seem to be mind-boggling, it is because they are. The scientists could not have begun the project without the aid of powerful supercomputers.

Scientists expect that the genome project will eventually be able to give doctors the unprecedented ability to use gene therapy to cure diseases. Once they understand the differences in each individual's genetic makeup, they will be able to custom design drugs targeted for specific individuals.

Cloning

One of the most fascinating developments of the twentieth century took place in 1997, when Scottish scientist Dr. Ian Wilmut successfully created a cloned sheep. Taking a single cell from an adult sheep, Wilmut was able to create a baby lamb that was a clone. In other words, it had the exact same genetic information as the adult sheep. Wilmut named the clone Dolly.

Wilmut's clone opened new worlds of possibility for genetic science. Some people were thrilled with the advancement, seeing a way to prevent endangered animals from becoming extinct. Others, however, saw cloning as a dangerous new tool. Some envisioned a world where new people—clones—could be produced for potentially dangerous purposes.

Atom by Atom

Nanotechnology, the science of the tiny, emerged during the 1990s. This revolutionary technology involves the manipulation

of matter at the atomic or molecular level. The main unit of measure, the nanometer, is the width of three atoms. Scientists hope to someday build tiny devices, atom by atom, for use in miniaturized manufacturing, drug-delivery systems, and nano-computers. Researchers have discovered new types of carbon molecules called fullerenes. In May 1998, Richard E. Smalley and his colleagues at the Center for Nanoscale Science and Technology at Rice University in Houston, Texas, used fullerenes to create thin tubes with closed ends called nanotubes. The nanotubes were one hundred times stronger than steel, yet six times lighter. By the end of the decade, many organizations in the United States, Europe, and Japan were conducting research in nanotechnology.

Dolly was the first successfully cloned mammal in 1997. This successful cloning experiment appeared to open the doors to seemingly limitless possibilities for future genetic research.

In the 1990s computers became easier to use than ever before, and the Internet gave people the freedom of telecommuting or shopping online. In politics, Bill Clinton became the second president in United States history to be impeached. Unfortunately, there also seemed to be outbreaks of violence, resulting in terrible bloodshed in schools and terrorist attacks. Still, as the century and the millennium drew to a close, Americans showed great optimism for the future.

An Amazing Decade

The 1990s were a decade of great change. Americans had reason to be optimistic about the future. With the end of the Cold War, nuclear war no longer loomed as a likely threat. But the world was still dangerous. Americans learned that they still had much to fear from terrorists, at home as well as abroad. And too great a dependence on foreign oil meant that events in the troubled Middle East could cause serious economic problems for America.

The 1990s were a prosperous period for most Americans. The economy during the two administrations of President Bill Clinton grew healthier each year. Unemployment fell to low levels, as did inflation. Even so, there was still much work to be done to make sure that all Americans, regardless of race or sex, had equal access to education and job opportunities.

Still, there were many positive happenings during the decade. The nation and the world survived the Y2K transition and its accompanying hysteria without a problem. Amazing advances in medical science, such as a more profound understanding of the human genome, were made. Such breakthroughs promised that, in the coming century, Americans would live longer, healthier, and, potentially, happier lives.

Timeline

1990 On February 11, **Nelson Mandela** is freed from prison in South Africa; on August 2, Iraq invades Kuwait, beginning the conflict that will lead to the Persian Gulf War.

1991 On January 16, the United States and its allies begin a bombing campaign against Iraq, which marks the start of the Persian Gulf War (led in part by **Norman Schwarzkopf**); on February 23, a ground invasion begins against Iraq; within one hundred hours, **Saddam Hussein** agrees to a cease-fire; on August 19, Communist hardliners try to oust Soviet leader **Mikhail Gorbachev**, but the coup is put down in part through the efforts of Russian President **Boris Yeltsin**; on December 25, the Soviet Union is dissolved; **Rodney King** is arrested and beaten by police in Los Angeles; **Tiger Woods** becomes the youngest winner of the United States Junior Amateur championship; the Yugloslav Army launches an attack against Croatia.

1992 On April 29, riots break out in Los Angeles after the police officers accused of beating Rodney King are acquitted; on November 3, **Bill Clinton** is elected president. **Bosnian Serbs** begin campaign of "ethnic cleansing"; White South Africans vote to end rule by whites by 1994.

1993 On February 26, Muslim terrorists bomb the World Trade Center in New York City; on February 28, a violent clash takes place between federal agents and members of the **Branch Davidian** cult in Waco, Texas; on April 19, the Branch Davidians die when they set fire to their housing compound; on September 13, Israeli leader **Yitzhak Rabin** and Palestinian leader **Yasir Arafat** sign historic peace accords in Washington, D.C.; on October 4, Russian President Boris Yeltsin's troops put down a revolt by former legislators; **Nelson Mandela** and South African President **F. W. de Klerk** share the Nobel Peace Prize; **Steven Spielberg** releases **Jurassic Park** and **Schindler's List**.

1994 On April 29, South Africa holds its first free elections, in which Nelson Mandela is elected president; in June, **Nicole Brown Simpson** and **Ron Goldman** are murdered, starting the O. J. Simpson murder case; in August, major-league baseball players go on strike; on November 8, Republicans win control of both houses of Congress and announce sweeping legislation called the Contract With America; on December 11, Russia begins a war with separatists in Chechnya;

Hutu officials in Rwanda organize a massive genocidal attack on the Tutsi people; musician **Kurt Cobain** commits suicide; in August, a twenty-fifth anniversary Woodstock concert is held in New York State.

1995 On March 20, a cult in Japan releases nerve gas in a Tokyo subway; on April 19, **Timothy McVeigh** bombs the Alfred P. Murrah Building in Oklahoma City; on October 3, **O. J. Simpson** is found not guilty of murdering ex-wife Nicole Brown Simpson and Ron Goldman; on November 4, Israeli leader **Yitzhak Rabin** is assassinated; on December 14, a treaty is signed to end war in Bosnia.

1996 On April 3, police arrest **Theodore Kaczynski**, the suspected Unabomber; on July 27, a bombing takes place in Atlanta, Georgia, at the Summer Olympic Games; on November 5, **Bill Clinton** is reelected president; on December 12, **Madeleine Albright** becomes the first woman secretary of state; South Africa passes a new constitution to protect equal rights; **Toy Story** premieres in theaters; **Tiger Woods** wins the PGA title and is named the tour's outstanding rookie; Baltimore Oriole **Cal Ripken, Jr.**, sets a record for playing in consecutive games.

1997 **Tiger Woods** becomes the first African American to win the Masters Tournament; on August 31, **Princess Diana** is killed in an automobile accident; President Bill Clinton's affair with White House intern **Monica Lewinsky** comes to light; **Titanic** premieres in theaters.

1998 On January 22, **Theodore Kaczynski** pleads guilty; in June, armed conflict breaks out in Kosovo; **Mark McGwire** and **Sammy Sosa** break Roger Maris's 1961 record of 61 home runs in a season; on December 19, **Bill Clinton** is impeached by the House of Representatives; **Saving Private Ryan** premieres; global warming concerns become more urgent, as 1998 is the warmest year ever recorded.

1999 On February 12, the Senate acquits **Bill Clinton**; in March, United States and allied troops start an air war over **Kosovo** and **Serbia**, which brings an end to the fighting there by June; on April 20, two high school students kill twelve other students, a teacher, and themselves at **Columbine High School** in Littleton, Colorado; **Tiger Woods** wins eight PGA tournaments in one year; **Tori Murden** becomes the first American and woman to row across the Atlantic Ocean; in December, researchers announce completion of the **Human Genome Project**; on December 31, **Y2K** fears prove unjustified.

Further Reading

Books

Avasthi,Smita. *Day by Day: The Nineties.* New York: Facts On File, 2003.

Gaines, Ann Graham. *Nelson Mandela and Apartheid in World History.* Berkeley Heights, N.J.: Enslow Publishers, Inc., 2001.

Holden, Henry. *The Persian Gulf War.* Berkeley Heights, N.J.: Enslow Publishers, Inc., 2003.

Jennings, Peter, and Todd Brewster. *The Century.* New York: Doubleday, 1998.

Kallen, Stuart A. *The 1990s.* San Diego, Calif.: Greenhaven Press, Inc., 2000.

Konemann Staff. *Decades of the 20th Century: The 1990s.* New York: Konemann, 2001.

Schuman, Michael A. *Bill Clinton.* Berkeley Heights, N.J.: Enslow Publishers, Inc., 2000.

Internet Addresses

Thunder and Lightning—The War With Iraq

http://www.history.navy.mil/wars/dstorm/ds5.htm

The Long Walk of Nelson Mandela

http://www.pbs.org/wgbh/pages/frontline/shows/mandela/

William J. Clinton

http://www.whitehouse.gov/history/presidents/bc42.html

Index